THE WORLD OF NASCAR

LIFE IN THE PITS:
Twenty Seconds That
Make the Difference

TRADITION BOOKS™
EXCELSIOR, MINNESOTA

BY JAMES
BUCKLEY JR.

Published by **Tradition Books**™ and distributed to the
school and library market by **The Child's World**®
P.O. Box 326
Chanhassen, MN 55317-0326
800/599-READ
http://www.childsworld.com

Photo Credits
Cover and title page: Sports Gallery/Tom Riles
Allsport: 8, 28 (Jonathan Ferrey); 22 (Jamie Squire); 26 (Chris Stanford)
AP/Wide World: 15, 16, 21, 27
Sports Gallery: 1, 19 (Tom Riles); 5 (Joe Robbins); Al Messerschmidt
   (9, 10, 14, 17, 20, 25); 13 (Brian Spurlock); 24 (Brian Cleary)

Book production by Shoreline Publishing Group, LLC
Art direction and design by The Design Lab

Library of Congress Cataloging-in-Publication Data

Buckley, James, Jr.
   Life in the pits : twenty seconds that make the difference / by James Buckley, Jr.
      p. cm. — (The world of NASCAR series)
   ISBN 1-59187-008-9 (lib. bdg. : alk. paper)
   1. Stock car racing—United States—Juvenile literature. 2. Pit crews—United States—
Juvenile literature. 3. NASCAR (Association)—Juvenile literature. [1. Pit crews. 2. Stock car
racing. 3. NASCAR (Association)] I. Title. II. Series.
   GV1029.9.S74 B84 2002
   796.72—dc21   2002004647

Printed in the United States of America.

L I F E   I N   T H E   P I T S

Table of Contents

INTRODUCTION

It's All about Teamwork

Have you ever heard the expression "life is the pits"? It means that things aren't going very well. You feel like you're in a big hole or pit. About twenty people on every stock-car racing team spend their whole life in the pits. They love every minute of it.

The "pit" and "pits" are the names auto racers use for the area where the cars pull in to gas up during a race. These breaks in the action are called "pit stops." They are handled by the members of the pit crew, who go over "**the wall.**" These highly trained specialists are just as important to the success of a stock car as the driver. Without a good, fast pit crew, a driver can't hope to win, no matter how fast his car is.

Just like your family car, stock cars need to fuel up. They need new tires and mechanical adjustments. They need all

sorts of other service to keep them running. Your family car can spend the day in the shop. Your parents can take 10 minutes to pull into a gas station and fill up with fuel. Stock car drivers, however, don't have the luxury of time during the heat of a race.

Every second a driver spends in the pits is a second they're not on the track racing full-out. The race doesn't stop when a driver goes into the pits. It just roars on around him. A driver in first place

Pit Row is one of the most colorful and action-packed places in racing.

before a pit stop can be in the back of the pack after one. Speed is just as important in the pits as it is on the track.

In stock car racing's early days, pit crews were friends of the drivers who knew a few things about cars. They were happy to be close to the action, and they often were learning as they worked. Today, because of the importance of speed, pit crews are professional. Each member has a specialty, and all the crews train long and hard to perfect their craft.

How fast do you think the very best pit crews in NASCAR can fill a car with fuel, change four tires, and get the driver some water?

Two minutes?

One minute?

The answer is less than 20 seconds! It can even be less than 15 seconds if they only change the two left-side tires. It took you longer to read this chapter than it does for a pit crew to do its job. Now that's racing!

CHAPTER ONE

Every Second Counts

For a NASCAR team, reaching Victory Lane on Sunday takes many hours of hard work. For pit crews, it means practice, practice, practice. Most teams practice at least three times a week. They are working to lower their times and still get the job done safely. They also work on training their bodies for the grueling work. This means lifting weights and doing other exercises.

It's nearly a full-time job for most of the crew members. Some also have other duties with the team. Many are highly trained mechanics who also work under the hood or on another of the car's systems. Some teams also have a pit crew leader who does nothing but train the crew and schedule workouts. Drivers practice with the crew regularly as well.

"Teamwork is everything in our sport," says the **crew**

chief for Jeremy Mayfield's number 19 Dodge Intrepid R/T, Sammy Johns. Pit crews in NASCAR are like the players in major league baseball. Team members have spent years working their way up to the top. They start out in smaller races and build their skills and knowledge. Pit crews are so important and popular now that there are even schools that train pit specialists.

The crew chief leads the team on and off the track. He guides the team's training and strategy. During the race, he sits on a small platform above the team. He watches the cars and gets information from all directions.

"I use a monitor that keeps track of every car in the race," says Sammy. "Also, it tells me where each car is in every lap

Crew chief Sammy Johns guides driver Jeremy Mayfield's car from the pits.

and how many laps have been run. It tells me everything I need to 'call the race.'"

The pit crew isn't the only one depending on the chief. "There's a lot of cheerleading involved [with the driver]," Sammy says.

"They're out there for 500 miles (805 kilometers) all by themselves and I'm the only person they can talk to. You have to encourage them sometimes."

The crew chief also consults all his experts and decides when to "pit." These decisions can often mean the difference between winning and losing. A lot of thought goes into just when to bring the car in.

"You can do all the planning you want before a race," laughs Sammy. "But it all seems to go out the window by the

Pit crews use computers and sharp eyes to help them run a great race.

A NASCAR official (white shoes, front) oversees a pit crew in the middle of a pit stop.

time the **green flag** drops [to start the race]."

Sammy and other crew chiefs have to decide 20 laps ahead of time when they'll pit. Teams also like to pit during **yellow flag** caution laps. These periods occur when there is an accident. The drivers must slow down and race in order while debris is cleared off the track.

Making the wrong choice about when to pit can mean waving goodbye to Victory Lane. Making the right one can mean a big post-race celebration. Life in the the pits is difficult, but pit crew members wouldn't trade it for anything.

CHAMPIONSHIP PIT CREWS

NASCAR drivers win on the track. Their crews win in the pits. While drivers get dozens of chances for victory, there's only one World Pit Crew Championship. In 2001, the team for driver Matt Kenseth took home the top prize. Matt's team changed four tires and refueled the car in only 17.695 seconds.

"That's incredible," wrote stock-car legend Richard "the King" Petty on Nascar.com. "I know guys who take that long to get out of their recliners and walk across the room!"

The annual competition tests a crew's ability to do their job quickly . . . and perfectly! No recliners allowed!

C H A P T E R   T W O

Swappin' Rubber

T ires are one of the key areas that crews concentrate on during a pit stop. These high-tech treads help hold a car to the track at high speed. They also help the driver grip the road during tight, high-banking turns. Tires are important to helping the car get the best **aerodynamics** by running evenly.

Seven pit crew members can hop over the low wall that separates the pit driving area from the crew area. Four of those pit crew people do jobs that involve changing tires.

The front- and rear-tire changers replace tires on the front and back of the car. They start with the right side, the side farthest away from the pit wall. Tire changers use special **air guns** to remove the five **lug nuts** that attach the wheel to the car. These guns can unscrew lug nuts in just over a sec-

ond. Zing, zing, zing, zing, zing . . . almost as fast as you can read that, the lug nuts are off.

Front- and rear-tire carriers help the tire changers. Tire carriers are the strong men of the pit crew. They heave 80- to 90-pound (36 to 41 kilograms) tires around like you flip a donut. The tire carriers hop over the wall carrying the tires and race to the right side of the car. The instant the tires are

Tire carriers and tire changers work together like ballet dancers to "swap rubber."

off, they hang the tires and "index" them. This means to line up the bolts on the car with the holes in the new wheel.

The lug nuts are glued to the new wheel. That way, the tire changer can just use his air gun to tighten the new nuts and, bam, they're done. These two mini-teams of carrier and changer then race around to the left side of the car and do it all over again.

"It's very choreographed," says Sammy Johns. "It can be almost a like a ballet. You've got these big tires, running men, and the flying hose of the air gun."

Other crew members who don't go over the wall assist the changer and carrier. They hand over new tires and retrieve the

Five lug nuts surround the center of each tire. Tire carriers line them up to bolts on the car's wheel.

used tires. They also pull the air gun hoses so that they don't get tangled. There's a fifth member of the tire changing team who is vital to the whole pit stop—the **jack man.**

"He's the key," says Johns. "The driver's signal to leave the pits is when the jack drops. If they don't have all their lug nuts on and the jack man drops it anyway, the driver's going. He's the quarterback of the team over the wall."

The jack man uses a 6- to 7-pound (2.7- to 3.2-kilogram)

The jack man (right of center) prepares to drop the
jack and release the driver.

aluminum jack. The jack is a device that lifts one side of the car completely off the ground. NASCAR jacks need only one or two pumps of a long handle. The jack man has to be big and strong to make it work just right. If there are any slip-ups, his team loses time. The jack man is the first person to reach the car. No one can work until he's gotten that jack working. Then he oversees the tire changers. When they're done and safe, he drops the car and the driver squeals back into action.

A tire changer flings his air hose as he races to the left side of the car to work.

WHERE THE RUBBER MEETS THE ROAD

To even the playing field, all teams in NASCAR use the same tires, all supplied by Goodyear. Because the tires are the same, it's important to know when to change them. One thing that teams look for is tire wear. To find out how the tires are wearing, they look at special "wear pins" that are inserted into each tire. More of the pin is exposed as the tire tread wears down.

To measure the pins, it's time to pull out a blowtorch. Crew members heat up the rubber buildup on the pins and scrape it from around the wear pin. That pin has been pre-measured. A new measurement is taken and that determines the tire wear.

Keeping track of a race team's many tires is almost a full-time job.

CHAPTER THREE

Gas and Go!

The other key area for pit crews is fuel. Without gasoline, that race car—or any car—would go nowhere fast. Pit crews have to make sure the car has enough fuel to get around the track and finish the job. Numerous drivers have seen victory disappear as they coast to a stop on the side of the track with an empty gas tank.

Two members of the over-the-wall team are responsible for fueling up the car. All NASCAR teams use special Unocal 76 high-**octane** gasoline. The gas man carries an 11-gallon (42-liter) gas tank over the wall. He puts the can's nozzle into a special fuel port at the back left side of the car.

Meanwhile, his partner, the **catch-can** man, inserts a special tool into a vent at the rear of the car. This action allows a fast and free flow of gas into the tank. He also holds

The two-man fueling team is seen at the bottom left
of this overhead photo.

a catch-can to grab any fuel that spills, keeping it off the track. The catch-can man then holds the first can while the gas man goes back for a second can. When the first can is empty, in goes the second can. As with anyone who works around dangerous chemicals, safety is a major concern of pit crews, especially the gas team.

"Fire is the worst thing we can have happen in the pits," says Sammy Johns. "We take every precaution. The gas man and catch-can man wear gloves and standard helmets like drivers. Their helmets also have fans blowing air in through vents. All seven guys who go over the wall also wear a full fire suit. They also have fireproof underwear and shoes. A new rule also says that all the crew members have to wear helmets."

Space man? No, gas man. Special fire suits protect crew members from fumes and flame.

DRIVER SERVICE

While the pit crew spends all its time making sure the race car is ready to rock, what about the driver? Who takes care of him?

That's the pit crew's job, too, but only once during a race. A NASCAR official in each pit lets a team know when it can "service the driver." That means that a pit crew member can hold out a new water bottle to the driver on a long pole. The driver swaps the new bottle for the old one in his in-car drinking system.

As for food, drivers don't eat during the race. They need both hands to drive. Also, they use up so much energy and sweat so much they don't have to go to the bathroom.

At the same time, another crew member reaches out with a squeegee to clean off the front windshield. If you see how many bugs end up on your car, imagine how hard it is for bugs to get away from cars going 150 miles per hour (241 kilometers per hour)!

Long poles reach from behind the wall to clean the grill, wipe the windshield, and help the driver.

Knowing when to put in fuel and how much to use is another crucial decision left up to the crew chief. "We keep track of the fuel use in the pits," says Sammy Johns. "The driver has a fuel pressure gauge in the car. All the drivers I've worked with never look at it, though. We have a technician who does nothing but keep track of fuel mileage during the race.

"To make sure we're putting in enough fuel, we use a computer program. We also use a calculator and count laps. We weigh the fuel before and after the pit stop. That tells us how much we got in the car on the last stop. Then we work out miles per gallon and laps per gallon. That tells us how much fuel we have left in the car."

This fiery flare-up shows how dangerous life in the pits can be.

C H A P T E R   F O U R

Pit Stop Step-by-Step

As soon as a driver reaches the pits, another kind of race starts. Here's how the action goes (take a deep breath!). The crew chief and driver decide that it's time to pit. Then the driver heads toward the special pit entry way off the main track. At most ovals, this is just before the final turn. A driver has to plan this move many miles ahead of time so he's in the right position to head onto pit row. As he enters pit row, he has to lower his speed to 45 miles per hour (72 kilometers per hour).

The driver heads to his designated pit area. The areas for all 43 drivers in the race are lined up along the main straightaway. The mad, colorful scramble of pit crews in different uniforms makes for one of the most exciting spectacles in a race.

A crew member holds up a large sign with a driver's car

number to show him where to stop. The driver has to stop his car within inches of his marks on the pit road track. Missing his mark by only a little bit costs valuable time.

The over-the-wall pit crew members can hop over the moment their car is one pit stall away from the mark. The jack man leads the way to the right side. With a couple quick pumps, he has the side of the car off the ground. The tire carriers heave the new tires over the wall and follow. The tire changers, pulling the air gun hoses and carrying the air guns, head to their tires, and start loosening nuts.

That blur is Jeff Gordon sliding to a stop at his position on Pit Row.

Watching over all this is a NASCAR official. He makes sure all teams follow the pit row rules. Penalties for the wrong equipment or procedures can cost a driver time or laps.

Meanwhile, the gas man and catch-can man are already pouring in the first tank. If it's a driver-service stop, a long pole stretches out from behind the wall with a water bottle. Another long pole reaches out to wash the windshield. A third pole can also come out and scrub the front grille. Air flow through the engine is crucial to keeping it cool. Anything stuck in the grille has to be removed.

The crew, in black, leaps over the wall as their driver approaches. Long poles hold target signs for the driver.

"It takes as many as 18 people to run a race," says Sammy Johns. "We couldn't do the job without all of them."

While all this is going on, the driver is taking a breath, getting ready to get back on the track. He won't get out of the car for the entire race, which can last five hours or more. Back on the track, other cars are zooming around, trying to gain time and distance on the racers in the pits.

The jack man zips around to the left side. There, the tire changers do their ballet again. The gas man finishes up and jumps back. The hoses are pulled back over as the left-side lug nuts are tightened. The jack drops, the tires squeal, the

All seven crew members are hard at work changing tires and putting in fuel.

crowd roars! The driver races back onto the track—and the pit crew takes a deep breath. They're exhausted.

This entire chapter happened in less than 20 seconds.

It's a lot of hard work, but there's a reward for pit crews. "There's no better feeling than winning on Sunday," says Johns. "After all the hard work these guys put in during the six days before the race, there's nothing better than to go to Victory Lane to celebrate."

The pit crews can handle that—no matter how tired they are.

All the hard work pays off! Bobby Hamilton's crew races to Victory Lane at Talladega in 2001.

BODY WORK

A basic pit stop fuels the car and changes tires. Thousands of other things can go wrong with a car, however. Pit stops are the way a team fixes them.

"We replace or fix broken or missing parts of the body more than anything else," says Sammy Johns. "Aerodynamics are so important in today's racing that you can't afford to lose speed because of a missing part."

Teams can replace hoods, fenders, noses, rear spoilers, and more in very little time. Crew members also can use big hammers to straighten out bumps or dents. For serious repairs, the car can be taken off the track into the garage. There a team can replace a transmission or gear box or do other big jobs. Even though this means there's no way a team can win, every lap counts for points. Teams want their car to be on the track as much as possible.

Sometimes crew members just need muscle. Here, they start to fix Jeff Gordon's dented car.

A DAY IN THE PITS

:00   Pit crew goes "over the wall"

:02   Jack man reaches right side of car and jacks it up

:02   Catch-can man opens vent; gas man begins pouring in fuel

:03   Front tire changer removes lug nuts

:04   Jack man removes right front tire; rear tire changer removes lug nuts

:05   Catch-can man holds first gas can; gas man goes for second

:06   Front tire carrier hangs new tire; rear tire carrier hangs new tire

:08   Rear tire changer tightens lug nuts; front tire changer tightens lug nuts

:09   Gas man puts in second can of fuel

:10   Jack man lowers right side of car and races around rear end

:13   Jack man raises left side of car

:14   Gas man finishes second can and he and catch-can man back away

:15   Rear tire changer removes lug nuts from left side

:16   Rear tire carrier hangs new tire

:16   Front tire carrier hangs new tire

:18   Rear tire changer tightens lug nuts

:18   Front tire changer tightens lug nuts

:20   Jack man lowers left side of car and pulls jack out from under car

:21   Driver accelerates out of pits

GLOSSARY

aerodynamics—the science of how air flows over an object

air guns—drill-like devices that use air pressure to turn and remove lug nuts

catch-can—a device used by a crew member to keep gas from spilling onto the track

crew chief—the person in charge of all crew members, on and off the track

green flag—the flag that signals the start of a race

jack man—the crew member who uses a long-handled aluminum jack to raise one side of the car

lug nuts—heavy, circular iron pieces that hold the wheels to the cars; NASCAR teams use five of them on each wheel.

octane—a measure of how powerful a fuel is; NASCAR teams use 106 octane fuel; regular cars only use 85- to 95-octane gas.

"the wall"— the 3-foot (.9-meter) concrete wall dividing the pit crew area from the pit road track

yellow flag—the flag that signals a "caution" period in which all drivers must slow to the same speed and stay in their current order until the track is cleared for safety

FOR MORE INFORMATION ABOUT LIFE IN THE PITS

Books

Center, Bill. *Ultimate Stock Car*. New York: Dorling Kindersley, 2000.

McGuire, Ann. *The History of NASCAR*. Broomall, Penn.: Chelsea House Publishers, 2000.

Menzer, Joe. *The Wildest Ride*. New York: Simon & Schuster, 2001.

Owens, Thomas S., and Diana Star Helmer. *NASCAR*. New York: Twenty-First Century Books, 2000.

Web Sites

The Official Web Site of NASCAR
http://www.nascar.com
For an overview of an entire season of NASCAR as well as the history of the sport and a dictionary of racing terms. The site also has video of a pit crew in action.

Fox Sports Network
http://www.foxsports.com
Click on the checkered flag, then NASCAR to find more details about every NASCAR race.

The Daytona International Speedway
http://www.DaytonaInternationalSpeedway.com
The official site of the most famous stock car track features maps of the track, information on buying tickets, and the history of the track.

INDEX

ABOUT THE AUTHOR

James Buckley Jr. has written more than 30 sports books for young people, on subjects including baseball, football, soccer, hockey, and basketball. He has worked for *Sports Illustrated* and NFL Publishing and was the editor of several childrens' magazines. He wishes that his local gas station was as fast as a real pit crew.